WILD EARTH

WILD EARTH
& Other Sonnets

Poems by

Cindy Ellen Hill

Antrim House
Bloomfield Connecticut

ISBN: 978-1-943826-96-4

First Edition, 2022

Printed & bound by Ingram Content Group

Book design by Rennie McQuilkin

Front cover painting by Katie Hoyt Carleton

Author photograph by Kristy Dooley

Antrim House
860.217.0023
AntrimHouseBooks@gmail.com
www.AntrimHouseBooks.com
400 Seabury Dr., #5196, Bloomfield, CT 06002

To my Dad, who liked to walk out in the woods

ACKNOWLEDGMENTS

Grateful acknowledgment to the editors of the following publications in which these poems first appeared, at times in earlier versions:

Minison Project Biannual Sonnet Journal, Spring 2021: "These Woods Are Mine"

Mountain Troubador 2021: "Seeing Champ" (2nd Place, Carol Lee Vail prize, Poetry Society of Vermont, 2021)

The Lyric, Summer 2021: "G Pentatonic, Maine Pine," Laureates' Choice winner in the 2021 Maria W. Faust Sonnet Contest

The Lyric, Winter 2021: "My Neighbor Is a Property Rights Man"

Classical Poets Society, online 2020: "Plum Island Solstice," "Climate Fire"

Classical Poets Society Best Poems of 2020, 4th Place: "Plum Island Solstice"

Ancient Paths, online December 2020: "All Divinity Is Love or Wonder"

Poetry Matters, December 2020: "Silver Solstice"

TABLE OF CONTENTS

I stand for what I stand on.
Edward Abbey

WILD EARTH

Ordinary Days

I awake and stretch, creaking with age;
no lover's hand to stroke my folds of flesh,
no devoted soul whose prayers embrace
my body, name me beautiful and blessed.

There is only the cold dawn, and a note
saying the coffee's on; yesterday's bread
unwrapped beside the words my husband wrote,
and on the floor an unwound spool of thread

the cats have battered through the house all night,
a tangled drunkard's path of passing years
meandering through beams of rosy light.
Picking up, my eyes grow hot with tears,

seeing through the early morning haze
the miracle of ordinary days.

Watering the Garden in Full Sun

Never water the garden in full sun.
Like magnifying glasses, droplets bead,
amplify the light and burn holes in the leaves.
Better to wait until the day is done
and cool dim light of evening has begun
before quenching that thirst that all life craves.
A drenching to the roots gently persuades
buds of even toughest thorn to open.

Our love should never see the light of day,
as it could never bear the scrutiny.
Imagined blossoms would all come undone,
drop petals in the wind to float away,
raked up with the scrumble and debris,
piled with the branches we have broken.

Let Us Sculpt This Morning Out of Beauty

Let us sculpt this morning out of beauty;
let us chip away the gloom of night
and cast the dust of yearning, loss and fright
upon the workshop floor, swept away.

Let us paint over words we said in anger;
let us erase the sorrow from this glade
and set our easels in the dappled shade
and sit enraptured by the bees and flowers.

Were we to sing of twilight, while the gold
descends through amber, salmon, purple, ebony
until owl's call supplants the day's cacophony,
our song would bid bright starlight to unfold.

Let us in courage wander hand in hand
and seed our wild creation through this land.

These Woods Are Mine

These woods are mine. I know the trail. I trace
the line of every snail that leaves a shine
along the cracked rock eaves over the race
of water cold and black beneath the pine.

I wait. I see the sunlight on the ferns,
the dappled flight of mayflies flit on morning
mist that glides above the stream and turns
between, like dreams that vanish, wakening.

My house is here. It does not need a gate
to lead the moose to moss, nor sign for deer
to find green growing shoots when spring comes late
and winter fails to loose its vines of fear.

I sleep. The crows return from where they've flown.
I lay my bones among the roots and stone.

Wild Earth

I dream in early darkness of a wild
earth, a land alive, a lithic hand to
hold my wild soul, sylvan pools that sing
of pregnant passion, maiden's blush of rose
in meadow bare upon the morning's breast.

Waking in the woodland glade I watch them,
watch the living, furred and flying, growing,
walking, soaring, stalking—watch and wonder
willingly, while willing You to whisper;
waiting for a word of reason, for cause,

for season, what would be the start or end,
between works of creation and of men.
Drinking in the dawn's breath I embrace them;
Unlike Adam, I refuse to name them.

In Praise of Weeds

Grass among the roses, ox-eye daisies
blooming 'round green cabbages and corn,
vex the gardener's eye and arouse scorn
in those who seek to order earth and sky,

who plant in rows—sterile, square and neat.
Violets and purslane won't emerge
for those who separate pathways from verge
and curse the wildness springing at their feet.

So much depends upon the hum of bees,
dancing, pointing, soaring o'er the vetch,
from elder, currant, vine and basswood trees

to dandelion, clover, rue and sedge.
So let us, rather, sing in praise of weeds
and everything that grows along the edge.

My Neighbor Is a Property Rights Man

My neighbor is a property rights man
who built his house right flush up to the line
because, he says, you know what's mine is mine;
zoning laws be damned—this is my land.

My neighbor plays his music turned up loud
and dumps his tires and brush over the fence.
To dispose of them on his lot gives offense
to his freedom. He will not be cowed.

I suppose it's fair, as after all,
I blare my silence and my buzzing bees
at him. I waft my scented garden breeze

in his direction; hold his home in thrall
to my lilac hedge and trellised beans,
dauntless constituting my demesne.

Seeing Champ

Lapping at the shore, the moon-road shimmers.
Dark shape glides deep enough to leave no wake,
flows down below the line of sight, then breaks
the surface—rising arc of gold glimmers.

This image seared in mind's eye clear as day:
Elegant curved neck, majestic eyes
locked on to yours, with all that look implies;
all that you were before now washed away.

To mention what you've seen is a mistake
you'll not repeat. The look on peoples' faces
shames you, casts you out of their good graces.
Silent, you drop your nets into the lake.

With each hauling-in, feel your grip wither.
Late each night, alone, you reconsider.

(Champ is the reputed Lake Champlain monster.)

Queenie

Now the garden's blanketed with snow.
Mice run in their tunnels far below
the powdered cold; the rabbits in their warrens,
chipmunks snug inside their dens, the wrens

long flown. There's only kibble—dull, immobile—
and that damned round ball that holds a bell.

Lie down, oh hunter, rest before the fire
and warm your claws. All living things grow tired

when glass replaces screen and skies are grey
and night-dark silence creeps across the day.
A hearth-nap does not mean you're growing old.
Unwind your pouncing-spring, and dream of bold

unbounded leaps when green, awake, returns
to your deep watchful lair beneath the ferns.

G Pentatonic, Maine Pine

The note had always been inside the flute—
just as the flute had been inside the tree
until the day that Two Bears cut it free
from newly fallen bole, down near the root
which, torn from earth, now pointed to the sky.
The tree had died a good death—wind, not knife,
the most that we can ask for in this life:
to have our souls rise on a gentle sigh
while everything inside us is released
into the air to flutter like a song,
in tunes that had been trapped there all along,
buried deeper as our years increased.

Sing now, flute, and set the sky alight
with joy, before the silent winter night.

Plum Island Solstice

I can see the Isle of Shoals across
the rock mouth of the Merrimac, where Thoreau
canoed two weeks, and mourned his brother's loss;
where fishing vessels roll, or wait to tow

unwary pleasure craft back into port.
A line of breaking waves marks the place
where river meets the sea, and just a short
way up the beach, seals on a jutting quay

bark and bray and stay just out of reach
of boys with pointed sticks who poke, oblivious
to mothers' scolding; for they cannot teach
a child of eight to see the obvious:

How swiftly turns the tide, how steep its toll,
how soft brown eyes can hold lost sailor's souls.

Shadow of a Crow

Against blue sky, high above May's budding
fringe of chartreuse mist, along a road
of placid lives where lawns are smoothly mowed,
battle to the death is fiercely raging.

Excoriating cries and beating wings—
two robins fly against a murderous foe,
pressing their attack, darting to and fro,
first diving, sharp claws bare; now barreling

upward as if they had been shot from slings.
Outnumbered and outsized, surely they know
the war was lost before they dealt one blow.

The enemy just let go. Their fledgling
plummeted to the pavement hard below,
its life lived in the shadow of a crow.

All Hallows Eve

Beeswax candle gutters in the wind
as drop by drop, long iron links of rain
descend the porch posts, seeking resurrection,
called back to natal ocean once again,

sliding eel-like over grassy plain,
amassing rivulets across the lawn
and pooling at the leaf-clogged driveway drain,
plummeting into dark earth, and gone.

All Hallows Eve, and ice will greet the dawn,
footing treacherous, split garden hoses—
hydrological phenomenon,
the way water expands when it is frozen,

the way that fear grows through each winter's night,
as souls await their summons to the light.

Standing in Rain

I have stood in pouring rain, soaked with fear
with sorrow saturating to my core,
drenched in everything that I abhor,
not blinking as my eyes begin to blear—
wet, yes, wet and cold, with no shelter near,
just listening to the thunder gods at war,
electric tension filling every pore
with sparkling blue, formed in a perfect sphere.

Catching my death, my mother used to say.
But she is gone, and I still stand in rain
whenever the gods deal out too much pain
for me to bear. I wash my sins away
upon the altar where raw nature reigns,
tattoos my skin, the watermark of Cain.

Landscape: Cliffs Above the Sea

Sometimes the cliff is made of solid rock.
Other times, it crumbles away softly—
grit and shale down-tumbling into the sea,
or fine sand pours off, steady, like a clock.
Sometimes on windy days I see the chalk
dust lifting in a cloud of pearly white,
wet pigments swirled against a slate grey sky.
Each drop of rain encapsulates a rock.

My heart erodes. Time cracks my soul, and ice
has slipped inside. Will it be fast, these last
years of my life, or slow collapse? Sometimes
I want to plant my feet and stand like gneiss,
iconographically, exert a vast
aesthetic influence, paint jagged lines.

A Man Riding a Bicycle

A man riding a bicycle without
a helmet through grey sheets of cold spring rain,
emitting joie de vivre, a dashing swain
defying elements, the type to flout
convention, not to mention law. He touts
an alteration of perception; grain
is not a thing to run along, and pain
and damp are things to consciously shut out.

A lesson here, I think, we learn from fools:
That life for everyone is not the same—
and recklessness or courage are but lenses
to look through as we read and write the rules
of navigating roads or other games
of chance. Perhaps we should drop pretenses,

realize our preconceptions are to blame,
admit we can not know the consequences.

Kin to All Who Whistle

These are the first notes of the aria:
the snap of chewing gum, a barking dog,
a tugboat churning past in midnight fog.
And now the chorus rises: *Gloria!*
Hosannah on high! Hallelujah!
How well we stumble deep into our grog;
footsteps tripping home, pipe-creaking frog,
street-dark laughter echoes: Euphoria.

No, no. We'll start again. The night is young
and we have yet to write where we have been.
Wine then, and piano. Clinking glass-notes
swirl, and songs emerge, whispered first, then flung
into the air, soaring past midnight, kin
to all who whistle as we don our coats.

In Nomine Meo

Carelessly indifferent to the seasons,
indifferent to the sigh of passing days,
not sighing as if lost in twilight greys
dreaming of a thousand fleeting reasons
years evaporate. Clouds of ripe melons
evaporate in early morning rain
like laughter flees the heart beset with pain.
Laughter beats in slow broad wings of herons—
even now they lift along the grey lake,
now lifting as the sun begins to rise,
hesitating, caught between two gold skies,
in gold asleep on water, and awake,
lingering along the heart's horizon—
light blooms, grey indifference forgotten.

April Is a Bully

April pries you loose from winter, kicks your fingers
off the icy ledge, forces you to look outside
as black-rutted frozen ground races to collide
with your too-soon-unbooted feet. Deep damp lingers.
Wind like the chill touch of a stalker sends shivers
down your spine. The shaking won't stop; though you've tried
to light the stove, the wood sputters. You slide
the match head twice, it smokes and dies. Your hands quiver.

April is a bully wearing an oversized
coat. It lasts exactly thirty days, the same
as many other months. Yet it does seem longer.
Ignore it, and maybe it will just quit, chastised,
dwindle away to languid green, mumbling your name
as if naming your survivors makes you stronger.

Jim Gallagher

Jim Gallagher bought about 36
wild acres back in 1985.
He was young then, and the land was near his
work. Outside among trees he felt alive.

The ground rises and falls. Everything does.

Like the stream cutting through rock ravine
and these sky-scraping stands of tall white pine.
He never thought those pines would ever lean
until they logged next door, up to his line.

The wind, the blow-downs; it's not like it was.

Jim walks each acre every single day,
rain or shine, sleet, cold, it makes no matter.
From here, this point of land, he can survey
the deer down in the browse, watch them scatter

when a rifle fires across the clear cut.

His own land is posted. There's the hemlocks,
where they bed down in deep snow. The fisher
cat likes to climb out on that branch, and fox
get in that brush, where all the rabbits are.

Every year the bear go for those beech nuts.

He picks up deadwood for the cabin stove.
He used to pull his water from the spring,
then they built a manufactory above
it on the hillside, cold black pipes leaking.

The ground beneath his boots rises and falls.
At night, in that old oak, the barred owl calls.

He found a fawn asleep behind that stone.
Out in these trees, Jim never is alone.

Small Against the Mountains

The barn appears small against the mountains—
a blood-red drop in an expanse of snow
that rolls unbroken through the fields below.
Bare trees rise beyond the silo, crowned in
sparkling morning ice. White-blue sky surmounts
forest and farm, holding spring in escrow.
On sagging fence-wire sits a single crow,
calling out that we must make allowance

for black emptiness behind the barn door.
Lichen on well-stones mirrors the mottle
of peeling paint on clapboards of the house.
Straw and glass lie scattered on the dirt floor,
skull and crossbones etched on broken bottle.
Pity the owl who eats the poisoned mouse.

Climate Fire

Charred brown stone. The odor of burnt roses,
red and lingering over desiccated
stems, dead leaves, beauty scarce abated,
even as its essence decomposes,

dissipates into the smoke that poses
as a summer mist, a scene created
as a reverie so long awaited,
castle where a shattered dream reposes.

This is how it is when fire rages
in a nation's soul. Denying facts
kills just as surely as the woodman's axe,

and yet despite the evidence, naught changes.
Perhaps this is the future we have earned,
where castles, vinyards, rose gardens can burn.

On the loss of Chateau Boswell in the Glass Fire,
California 2020

Roots of the Rowan Seed

Rowan seedling sprouted in the crevice
of a rock, deep beneath a hemlock grove,
high upon a hill without a name.
I am rooting for the rowan; it is
in my Celtic blood, although I have
no right to impose species bigotry;
this is not my garden, not my place
to lay a wager on the seed, the stone,

the shade, which one of them shall long prevail,
and which of them shall simply fade away;
which of the earth's endeavors shall see glory
far beyond the counting of my days.
Time never tells before the shadow fades
which monument shall stand, and which shall fail.

All Divinity Is Love or Wonder

(New Harbor, Maine October 2020)

All Divinity is love or wonder.
The moon pulls up the sea, while rocks plunge deeply
underneath: ragged, cracked asunder,
synclined metamorphic panoply.

Moonlight fractals over night-black surface,
crimson embers dance on dying coals.
A Fresnel beam each fifteen seconds passes,
warning of Monhegan Island's shoals.

Pulse and gentle pulse, the sea, the shore,
the turn of granite tide and melting stones;
waves erode the soul down to its core.
Pulse of wonder, cut by calling crows

navigating limbs of twisted pine.
Gnarled roots delve into the divine.

*"All divinity is love or wonder" is from "A Valediction
of the Book," 4th stanza, by John Donne*

November Sonnet

Persephone descends with joy to her
dark lover. Footsteps clatter in the stone
stairwell, scarlet gown billows and swirls,
hair streams out behind her as she runs.

Above, the hearth now burns all through the day.
Smell of baking bread seeps from the kitchen,
sage and garlic keep the chill at bay,
the stew is rich with venison and pumpkin.

Harvest fruit set up in glistening jars
like so many decisions yet unmade.
The woodsman's swinging axe makes him twice warm;
his thoughts his own, he whistles with the blade.

Below, the maiden tastes the seeds of bliss.
The night lord's kiss is sweet on her red lips.

Silver Solstice

Pale sun slides low across the silver sky
and weakly spins a thread of silver light
to hold the force of day against the night,
the all-entombing darkness to defy.
Like mycorrhizal filaments through earth
or water pulsing up through bedrock fault,
Light lives, though buried deep within a vault,
like seeds that slumber, dreaming of rebirth.
Silver mist of dawn slips through the oak,
envelops twigs of ash and birch and beech.
Silver tendrils slip and wrap and reach,
bright majesty of morning to uncloak.
      Though darkness wields each facet of its art,
      it cannot tarnish joy within our heart.

LIST OF SONNETS WITH SONNET TYPE

"Ordinary Days," English sonnet

"Watering the Garden in Full Sun," Italian sonnet

"Let us Sculpt the Morning Out of Beauty," Bowlesian sonnet

"These Woods Are Mine," English sonnet

"Wild Earth," Lannet sonnet with final rhyming couplet

"In Praise of Weeds," Italian form variation

"My Neighbor is a Property Rights Man,"
  Petrarchan sonnet variation

"Seeing Champ," Bowlesian sonnet

"Queenie," sonnet in rhyming couplets

"G Pentatonic, Maine Pine," Bowlesian sonnet

"Plum Island Solstice," English sonnet

"Shadow of a Crow," variation of a Four Kings sonnet

"All Hallows Eve," Spenserian sonnet

"Standing in Rain," Italian sonnet

"Landscape: Cliffs Above the Sea," Italian sonnet

"A Man Riding a Bicycle," caudated sonnet

"Kin to All Who Whistle," Italian sonnet

"In Nomine Meo," name acrostic Italian sonnet

"April Is a Bully," Italian sonnet in hexameter

"Jim Gallagher," Double interwoven English sonnets

"Small Against the Mountains," Italian sonnet

"Climate Fire," Italian sonnet

"Roots of the Rowan Seed," Lannet variation, unrhymed octet,
  Italian sestet

"All Divinity is Love or Wonder," English sonnet

"November Sonnet," English sonnet

"Silver Solstice," Bowlesian sonnet

ABOUT THE AUTHOR

Cindy Hill is an environmental attorney, writer, musician, and obsessed gardener living in Middlebury, Vermont. Her poetry has appeared in many publications and on National Public Radio. Composing music developed her appreciation of rhyme and meter, and she now writes primarily formal poetry, particularly sonnets.

This book is set in Garamond Premier Pro, which had its genesis in 1988 when type-designer Robert Slimbach visited the Plantin-Moretus Museum in Antwerp, Belgium, to study its collection of Claude Garamond's metal punches and typefaces. During the fifteen hundreds, Garamond – a Parisian punch-cutter – produced a refined array of book types that combined an unprecedented degree of balance and elegance, for centuries standing as the pinnacle of beauty and practicality in type-founding. Slimbach has created a new interpretation based on Garamond's designs and on compatible italics cut by Robert Granjon, Garamond's contemporary.

Copies of this book can be ordered
from all bookstores including Amazon
and directly from the author:
Cindy Ellen Hill
144 Mead Lane
Middlebury, VT 05753
Please send $12 per book
plus $4.00 shipping in the U.S.
and $6.00 beyond
by check payable to
Cindy Ellen Hill.

•

For more information on the work of Cindy Hill
visit www.antrimhousebooks.com/authors.html.

CPSIA information can be obtained
at www.ICGtesting.com
Printed in the USA
BVHW080751130222
628727BV00001B/58